I WAS NEVER ALONE

View of the Venice sky on a thunderstorm night clicked by the author in July, 2019

I WAS NEVER ALONE

Author
ARNAB NEOGI

GLOBAL INFLUENCERS PUBLISHING HOUSE
152 Prince Charles Cr, #17-12 Singapore 159013
Website: www.globalinfluencers.sg
Email: shikha@globalinfluencers.sg
First Published in Singapore by
Global Influencers Publishing House 2022

Title: I Was Never Alone
ISBN: 978-981-18-4211-5
MRP: US$13.99

GLOBAL INFLUENCERS PUBLISHING HOUSE

Printed and bound by Redflame Publishers

To my late sister who has been a
guiding light in my journey as a poet.

To Linus who will always be our guardian Angel.

And to Luna, so that she grows up to embrace the world
as one big family, knowing she is never alone!

Contents

About the Author

Arnab's journey as a poet span across two decades, during which he has dabbled in various poetry forms, although his writings are mostly in free verse.

He got his first major critical appreciation when one of his first poems "***Remembering the Dead***" (1998) appeared in the "*Inkspot*" column of The Pioneer Ltd. He published his first volume of poetry "***Inspiration***" (2007, Offset Printers, Lucknow, India). His second volume "***Beyond the Silver***

Lining... (ISBN 9789382393214, Sanbun Publishers, New Delhi, India, 2013) received positive reviews.

He has featured in more than a dozen anthologies of poetry. Eminent anthologies include "***Taj Mahal Review***" (Vol 11, No#2, Cyberwit.net Publishers, 2012), ***"Indus Valley" (***Xpress Publications, 2012), "***Muse India***" (Issue 49, 2013), "***Inklinks***" (ISBN 9788182533714, Cyberwit.net Publishers, 2013).

Arnab co-authored with his wife, a duet-poem "***Chapter Zero***" which was published in the world's first-ever duet poetry anthology "***Synthesis***" (ISBN 9789383770021, Xpress Publications, 2014) featuring a place in the Limca Book of Records. His literary memberships include the coveted "*World Poets Society*" and "*Indian Society of Authors*" (InSa, New Delhi).

Outside the world of poetry, Arnab works as Product Management leader for a US-based Fortune 500 manufacturing conglomerate. He currently resides in Hong Kong with his wife Olivia and daughter Luna.

Arnab Neogi can be contacted on:

LinkedIn: *https://www.linkedin.com/in/arnabneogi/*

Facebook: *https://www.facebook.com/arnab.neogi.9/*

Foreword

It is my pleasure to introduce the collection *'I was never alone'* by Arnab Neogi to all the readers. The principle theme of this work is assorted but the context of the book stays the same as the title.

In this book the poet talks about his journey and how people always had his back and that he was never alone. This book has been written in the span of 7-8 years but it expands to the life of the poet. The main content of the book demonstrates that a poet's journey is just like a common man's journey. Which makes it the most enjoyable and relatable. He demonstrates a common journey that every individual undertakes in their life. *'I was never alone'* is thus a song of joy and celebration of solitude.

I have known Arnab for quite some time and it is really heartening to see him come so far and evolve. This visionary journey has been expressed elegantly in the collection *'I was never alone'*. I hope that readers would find comfort and joy while reading this astonishing work.

Sandeep Nath

Eminent lyricist, composer, singer & screenwriter in Bollywood, the Indian film industry. Notable works include compositions in movies like 'Page 3', 'Saawariyan', 'Aashiqui 2', 'Roy', etc. Winner of Stardust Awards in 2008 & Mirchi Music Awards in 2014 and 2016.

1.

I Was Never Alone

I thought one day, dead tired from life,
What if somebody could listen to my silence?
And dispel the shroud of solitude from my soul,
Or, else curse me to eternal solitude;

I keep dangling in the middle unquestioned,
See images when lonely; turn blind amidst a human sea,
Was I ever alone, born and raised by two darlings?
I was never alone; I was indeed never alone;

I tirelessly searched for God amidst candid distractions,
And I delved deep only into a quicksand
Only to see the 'two darlings' pull me out,
Thence, I found God; and yes, was left sometimes alone;

I have written since the sand touched my feet,
And have only found repeating my life repeatedly

Words have eluded me, fogged away in front of my eyes,
And my thoughts have clouded over, no rain-drops yet;

Perhaps, in sunrises yet to come, I'll see the beings chirping,
Or, would in a gathering enjoy each other's silence
Lest someone remarks "He's still alone",
Smile, "No, I am not alone, I was never alone with my two darlings".

P.S: Dedicated to my parents for never letting me feel alone

2.

Amidst the Gory Bonhomie

Amidst the gory dark bonhomie of apprehensions,
There comes up a sweet vision of a hand forward,
Hand just extended to hold forever and walk,
Let's sit and talk, for there won't be a walk;

I grew up a fortune and never knew riches of innocence,
For the world was so busy piling hatred,
And then you gave birth to a fantasy,
Hand in hand we roll and we grew young together,

For it is not the world but our own
heart that breeds hatred;
Love be pure like innocence, let's grow a
grey streak together;

3.

The Knight in Shining Armour

Yes, amorous disdain in unclothed wine,
Tasted full throttle into your lap,
With years of charisma footloose
I sit back and look into her eyes,

Yes, into her kohl-rimmed eyes I look
And discover a hint of madness,
Similar to what Endymion saw in Selene
And in uncouth freedom, and nude spirits,

Yes, her nude spirits overwhelmed time
And I vowed to be her knight,
Interlace her beauty with dark red wine
Pour my love with full might,

She dazzled the objects around
I sit muted, awestruck and blade shining,

Dangling in absurd shows run aground
I could only hear, and feel her whining,

The clothes burn on our bodies
And we sit back liberated and easy.

4.

Humour

The slow bite tickles the bone,
And a deafening silence is broken,
Through ages the laughter was heard,
And now silence beckons thy lonely soul.

Gods do proclaim eternity of the soul,
Whilst humour doth remind mankind of mortality,
The dark humour beckons thy name,
Wish we were back to those laughing days.

Unfounded love shreds its bitter face,
The man and his woman string those bonds together,
And tries to hold on to that last bit,
Humour certainly rescues that crumbling love.

Laugh, and the world shall humour you,
Cry and our humour doth betray us to the grave.

5.

In Memory of Those Platonic Eroticism

That night.
The night fell and so did the lover,
Over bosoms lay bare until she sighed,
Relieved yet mistakenly frowning upon him,
"And what did I do which you didn't desire".

Warm air filled the place with dignity,
And she lost what she valued the most, her chastity!
Was this the lover or some stranger, she calculated,
Yes, the lover it was! The sighs did cast a mist.

A black swan flew over her head and her heart,
She perfected the art of misgivings and lied down,
The lover was blind and erotic,
And the black swan turned white above.

In the disaster of the dark,
Every man pledged love and loyalty to the wife;
How do I swear loyalty to her
When every other woman is the same?

A poetic conjugation is all that a heart needs
Under that philanthropic body which needs love,
From the echelons of time, woman loves a man
For that same happiness a sea bird swings across,

Dear girl, stay with me till the last word,
And let's swear some love out of the books.

6.

Those Little Rain-drops

Those little rain-drops.
Those little rain-drops splash on the wooden carcass,
Those dew-drops get swollen with envy,
As the sunshine beams on the sparkling drops,

Rain or dew, it's those drops after all, tear-drops?
Tell me Son, when those eyes ooze love,
And hope some return eyes,
Is there time for us to realize?

Maybe, we should stand united and love.
The little splatter of some drops on the parapet,
Which fell first?
Let's go about the exercise of drops,
And tears definitely would fall first.

Those little rain-drops shine incessantly,
And we are all wet with shower,
And some dew does quench our thirst,
And tears do quench our lonely hearts.

7.

I Sit Motionless

In a wide green expanse,
A knight in shining armour
Barks at the rain clouds above
And it grows dark with rain;

In a big grass of unfathomable depth
Stray souls go by in their errands
And I sit motionless in one corner
Within a lovely break from my routine;

With hunger I feel my appetite beckon,
Raise my hopes and dash instantly,
As I dream of roosting under grey puffs,
I stand, bearing this solitude;

I tremble at a single rain-drop,
Not sure to welcome it or let go,

In this haze of a blurred maze
My vision unfolds the truth;

I wake up to the green around
And still motionless, I sit.

8.

An Artist

I dream of art and perfection,
Each time I die and reclaim faith,
No! Not my audience but my inner self,
I love art and I am wounded, dear;

I wish I had sung that song
Or had written that piece,
And my voice as soft as Orpheus' music,
Alas! I am born in this era and I'll die soon;

Sometimes my country beckons and am martyred,
Sometimes my love beckons and all love's sacrificed,
Then my inner self calls loud,
And I want to be left alone to my fantasies;

Loud and clear an Artist's works shines,
Still louder is the plea of rejection.

9.

Alone I Dream

"Look darling, in loneliness I dwell and creek,
I shriek in hell and cry loud and the music
plays even louder,
Yes, I live in abject solitude sans the strings of music",
I grope and find the musical curves soothing my heart;

Wish I could sing that way,
The world would pay me gratitude for the song,
Alas! The song is slowly fading away,
As glasses clash and heads roll;

Darling, you left me so long ago,
Before I could ever stand up straight,
Or think straight or reconcile to the pungent truth,
A love blossomed and sparkled and faded too soon;

For all the music that bites my ears,
Let the fountain of youth befall us both
And grant us an ever-lasting intimacy,
Of fire-filled lust and education sans love;

"Look darling, in loneliness I dwell and creek,
And now am bit easy and light and
the music plays loudest,
Yes, these drops of liquor with an allied
art dispels solitude",
I bare it all and find the strings still vibrating;

Of true passion and accurate imagination,
I fight everything and fall back...alone I dream.

10.

A Mistake

I breathed slowly onto her blank face,
And lurched forward to touch her glowing cheeks,
And in a desperate march down,
I sighed and fell flat onto her bosom;

In another moment of heightened passion,
I painted the grey skies dark,
Until we could not see but only feel,
And I tasted the first love in a trance,

I realized only the sky draped me blue,
And wanted freedom from my own skin,
And so I hid in her skins, dismayed and appalled,
And latched onto the curves lest I roll down a cliff.

That the moment holds steadfast till I loosen,
How to transform a mistake into a boon?

11.

There Was a Time

There was a time in some medieval era,
When gold shone and blood dripped
When a worthless prince shivered in lust
And a useless slave shuddered in starvation;

There was a time in some ancient era,
When wheel started rolling and weapons made,
When a self-taught freeman instilled false moralities
And a true disciple pledged eternal knowledge;

But there is now a time in a pseudo-modern era,
When life is re-discovered in an isolated room,
When an audacious being makes his money talk
And the common man struggles in heightened
sense of duty;

As I travel across the unstoppable time
I would want to live and die out of destiny's time.

12.

The Heights of Infinity

There would be a time in furloughs
From the drone of civil work,
Where I lay down intoxicated and wet
Claiming to have a blurred glimpse of her;

And there would be those moments of mirth,
Candled by your light of innocence and love,
Cuddled by your smouldering breath
I lie down dizzy, warmed but not burnt;

Then again there be moments of truth,
Of crass infamy bundled by falsehood,
And I bow down and plead infidelity,
Your pure soul denigrates mine tomfoolery;

And there be those gory moments of silence,
Compounded by uncivil boundaries of expressions,

of love and lust alike, pain profound
At last I discover the sky above, blue and endless;

Now there be no moments of anything,
Simply sit back and tune to something familiar,
Yes, mind can extort from those facades
What was real was love indeed, I wait.

13.

A Song For You

The hot days and windy nights,
Bequeaths a treasure of spark,
Burnt desires ripen with music
And the wind blows off my feet;

In droplets of tears that heart sheds
The ink blurs and dabbles the words into solid colours,
Writings appear not on paper but on walls
And such words can't be sung or strummed;

Incompleteness and indistinct faces prick
And a song oozes out in pure red form,
The words recreates inside the mind
And gives birth to a child;

Every song is for you and words
That won't stir the past are these,

Every word is your formation
And the song remains to be sung sometime;

The triad of music words and memories
Beckon every lost second to come back,
And time on its wheels rolls constant
Shredded by that string that unites my song;

The dark love screams sans its reflection in words,
And the poet struggles to pen his thoughts
Before this moment is over,
Let's recollect some of those songs sung together.

14.

Ode to Journey

Time on its wheels and the chariot broke,
And thus time flew past in a shot unknown,
People dance and I raze my memory,
Yet I think, remember these two years hence;

It began and ended like in a trance,
Not a soul stirred, as it were deep asleep,
Beautiful men, women craved ignorance,
An ocean of heart melts tonight, cries out;

Never shall sing those unheard songs again,
The present slowly smouldering ashes
Upon charred tales of hallowed brotherhood,
The music shall die in a March retreat;

Ahoy! We multiply joy of journey,
Recreate the illusion years later,

In memories such as these incomplete,
Some new place where these voices rekindle.

15.

A Caustic Remark

Bloodshot eyes in a cold labyrinth,
The walls echo with silent reverberations
Of her caustic remark shot inside,
And I kick hard against the walls of my destiny;

I run, I walk and the echo vibrates
The essence of bitterness personified,
And I desperately search for sweetness
Where I trip into unheard voices;

I lie down and a wave runs across,
The caustic smell freshened the remark,
Of sweet fragrances from honeymoon days
Turned sour with years of words let loose;

A mind is swollen with swamps of solitude
Or is it a desert of cold fun? I die.

16.

Your World After Me

Love, what would be the world without me?
In some dark isolation the thoughts would not run wild,
Yet people would continue their lives,
And your world won't be the same without me.

Would you hold on to all that was loved and lost?
And care for the old and fill the void,
Or care for the baby and tell her my tales,
Yourself, remember the folklore and smile.

Love, when would you stop thinking
where it went wrong?
For there is everything right between you and me,
Destiny, that's what is wrong, and judgment,
But we can mend and be together again sometime.

Could I charge you with three-fold eternal duties?
To care for the old and fill the void,
Or care for the baby and tell her my tales,
Yourself, remember the folklore and smile.

Love, they say time heals the deepest wounds,
Let's wait for our time then?
Whilst the old relax, and the babies play,
Let's ruminate and make memories laugh.

17.

Abuse

Where do I go from here, dear?
Is there no place to come back to?
Surely there was once a moon that was silvery,
And love manifested as gentle abuse.

Where do I go from here, dear?
Is there no time to get back to?
Surely there was once a cuckoo that sang,
And care overly nurtured as gentle abuse.

Where do I go from here, dear?
Is there no memory to flee past?
Surely there was once a chrysanthemum that perfumed,
And compassion morphed into gentle abuse.

Where do I go from here, dear?
Is there no thing to cling on to?

Surely there was once a rain that splattered,
And tears were washed away, dried by gentle abuse.

For lovers never abuse, there isn't any boundaries,
To check love turning monstrous, and define abuse.

18.

A Little Romance

A little romance,
Feeling suppressed
And disordained
With careless disdain.

Dreams during each sleep,
Wakes up trembling
And wished to be sweet,
Then something calls aloud.

But nobody in sight,
Again I am alone
In a world of strangers,
I'll find a way.

Maybe I won't need a soul
I can't tell why I am happy still.

19.

My Brother

I look so intently into each eyes,
And behold the warmth from your heart,
Feel the absence of known faces,
Yet strangers get loved as brothers;

For the love of all that's holy,
Sip nectar and earn your brotherhood,
Every sunrise I vow to be civil,
Yet strangers get loved as brothers;

The girl beside that mound,
Looks upon intently with warm eyes,
And my soul races to hug her,
In deep seated love for the brother;

Man will never know how the warmth
will fade, I won't risk a woman or man.

20.

The Man Who Once Walked the Earth

Yes, he saw me take those first baby steps,
And I was destined to see his,
In a true oxymoron, time does take a full circle,
In life or in death; beginning or the end?

Yes, he saw me write those first words of eulogy
To the then departed, when his world crashed,
And lo! Now I write again when ours crashed,
In a true oxymoron, memories get constantly replaced.

It seemed as if he were on a hiatus,
A vacation from the drudgery of life,
But who would wish to return from Paradise,
Whence you find your own blood older than you,
Know, sooner than later be united again
with those you left.

There again, time now runs backwards,
And your child is your Mother,
But we gaze up and see the same face
Only to wonder, where have you gone?
And he looks around and replies "Everywhere dear!"

"You would find me everywhere, know where to look,
In deepest thoughts and loftiest joys,
In wildest fears and darkest sorrows,
I will partake, and you'll feel my touch,
Not everything can be seen, just remember me"

He came and went quickly, as time would have it,
In pain and in sorrow, left an indelible mark
On the sands of time,
The smell of the jasmine is life, and not death,
In life and in death, it's a human construct.

We who do understand this do not fear losing,
It is not a loss, but a gain
For either us or the Lord,
Someone would smile, someone would cry,
It's just another great balancing act.

And for the last time, I'm the new wordsmith
Born out of time,
With this old eulogy to the man who once walked the earth,
And will walk the Paradise now
In life and in death, reside beside the fountain of eternal joy!

P.S: This poem is dedicated to my late uncle in the hope he would still listen patiently to my recitals.

21.

Ode To Linus

You were a ray of hope
Once, on a sunny morning,
The greatest gift of life
Is the creation of life itself;

You were a colourful shadow of joy
Once, when teardrops rain from Heaven,
The greatest bane of life
Is the burial of your creation itself;

Shall we depart your troubled body?
Free the spirit to the Other World,
Hope it returns to us someday
To bless and create life again;

Meanwhile, time shall stand still
And figures but frozen in cold apathy,

A man and woman can only question
Was it joy or a higher joy?

Devoid of all absurdities and distractions
Linus, you were the strongest bond
That bound our plural world,
You breathed inside, yet calmer outside that day;

"It will always be a journey, Son
From one world to the other",
And till you are with HIM
Know that you reside in our hearts too

P.S: This poem is dedicated to Linus, our greatest gift

www.ingramcontent.com/pod-product-compliance
Lightning Source LLC
LaVergne TN
LVHW010506160826
845677LV00012B/2687

* 9 7 8 9 8 1 1 8 4 2 1 1 5 *